Once upon a time there was a great big lion and a tiny little mouse.

One day the little mouse was looking for some food when she saw the lion lying under a tree.

The lion opened one eye and saw the little mouse.

He caught the little mouse in his paw.

'Please do not hurt me, Mr Lion,' the little mouse said. 'One day, I may be able to help you.'

The lion laughed and laughed but he let the mouse go.

'You are too little,' he said. 'You cannot help me.'

But the little mouse squeaked,

Some time later the lion was caught in a trap.

'Help, help,' roared the lion.

A monkey heard the lion roaring.

He saw the lion in the trap and he said,

The monkey tried and tried to help the lion. He scratched and scratched at the ropes but he could not get the lion out of the trap.

'Help, help,' roared the lion.

A snake heard the lion roaring. She saw the lion in the trap and she hissed,

The snake tried and tried to help the lion.
She tugged and tugged at the rope but she could not get the lion out of the trap.
'Help, help,' roared the lion.
An elephant heard the lion roaring.
He saw the lion in the trap and he trumpeted,

The elephant tried and tried to help the lion. He pulled and he pulled at the ropes but he could not get the lion out of the trap.

'Help, help,' roared the lion.

The little mouse heard the lion roaring. She saw the lion and she squeaked,

The little mouse gnawed and gnawed at the ropes.

Her sharp teeth cut through the rope and at last the lion was free.

'Thank you,' said the lion.

'You may be little but you can help.'

And the little mouse squeaked and said,

Yes, I can.